Reader's Digest
READING SKILL BUILDER

W9-ABB-392

SILVER EDITION EDITORS

Miriam Weiss Meyer and Peter Travers, Project Editors

Barbara Antonopulos and Jacqueline Kinghorn, Editors

SILVER EDITION CONSULTANTS

Fred Chavez, Director of Programs
Los Angeles City Reading Support Services Center
Los Angeles, California

Marguerite E. Fuller, Assistant Supervisor of Language Arts
Norwalk Public Schools
Norwalk, Connecticut

Sister Maria Loyola, I.H.M., Chairperson, Reading Curriculum Committee
Archdiocese of Philadelphia
Philadelphia, Pennsylvania

Dr. John. F. Savage, Coordinator, Reading Specialist Program
Boston College, School of Education
Chestnut Hill, Massachusetts

Richard B. Solymos, Reading Resource Teacher
School Board of Broward County
Fort Lauderdale, Florida

READER'S DIGEST EDUCATIONAL DIVISION
© 1977 by Reader's Digest Services, Inc., Pleasantville, N.Y. 10570. All rights reserved, including
the right to reproduce this book or parts thereof in any form.
Printed in the United States of America.
Reader's Digest ® Trademark Reg. U.S. Pat. Off. Marca Registrada ISBN 0-88300-411-9

■ ■ ■ **Part 1**

Silver Edition

STORIES

4

They Ride the Big Waves
What makes so many people love the dangerous sport of surfing?
RDX 97

12 **Old Cars Never Die**
The story of an old car that was sent to a junkyard—as told by the car itself! RDX 98

18 **Prairie School**
Spend a day in a one-room schoolhouse on the prairie. RDX 99

28

Mexico's Mysterious Lost City 🖭
What turned a once-great city into ruins in the jungle?
RDX 100

36 **The Unknown Artist**
Poor Archibald Willard. Hardly anyone remembers this unknown artist who created one of the most famous U.S. paintings—*The Spirit of '76.* RDX 101

45 **Teacher Robot** 🖭
When Mrs. Freeman needed a helper in her classroom, she brought in a robot, of course. RDX 102

🖭 Stories for which Audio Lessons are available.
RDX number indicates RDX card for that story.

51 | **A House That Runs on the Sun**
A thunderstorm shows Mr. Thomason a good way to heat his home—with sun power! RDX 103

58 | **The Remarkable Desert Zoo**
Where does the desert end and the zoo begin? Sometimes it's hard to tell. RDX 104

65 | **Monika Lou, Magician of the Flipped Disk**
Monika Lou made many new friends while playing Frisbee. She also became a world Frisbee champion. RDX 105

71 | **Bubbles Are Beautiful—And More**
These buildings are held up by nothing but air! RDX 106

78 | **James, the Marvelous Musician** 🖭
An Australian lyrebird gives his friendship to Mrs. Wilkinson and his magical beauty and voice to the world. RDX 107

87 | **The Long Sleep of Gene Tipps** 🖭
A bright college student, hurt in a car accident, stays half-conscious for eight long years. RDX 108

Key Words

surfer, surfing
Hawaii, Hawaiian
plastic

They Ride the Big Waves

by Eugene Burdick

If you were a doctor, would you give up your medical career and become a full-time surfer? A doctor in California did. Why? "The sea is part of all of us," he said. "It has a beauty that draws us to it. I want to enjoy the waves now. Later I'll go back to my medical career."

This doctor-surfer travels all over the world. He lives in a tent on the beach. He is always searching for waves called *the big ones*.

A wave is a strange thing. It starts far out at sea, where it may stand over ten stories high. But it doesn't break. That comes later.

The wave moves close to land. The water there isn't so deep. The power inside the wave has to go somewhere, so it pushes the water up. The wave climbs to a peak and then breaks. The mountain of water comes crashing down.

The shape of the beach shapes the waves. At some beaches, waves break in steep hills of foam. No smart surfer would ride waves like that. Other waves are long and gentle, and a surfer can safely ride a long way on them.

Very big waves called *heavies* come to the beaches of Hawaii. Only expert surfers try the heavies, for these waves can be very dangerous.

Pretend you're a surfer. Lie on your board and glance behind you. Ready? Choose your wave and begin pushing through the

Wipeout!

6

Hanging Five

water with your hands. When you get to the *hump* (top) of the wave, it's time to *take off*.

Stand up. See the long slope of the wave in front of you, and hear the hiss of the water as your board slices through the wave. A hill of water races after you. It sounds like thunder.

One wrong move, and you're in trouble. If you go too fast, the board will hurl itself out of the wave. You will go up in the air and then crash back into the water. Or you might fall off the board and be caught in a *wipeout*.

Shooting the Curl

7

Surfers know that only skill and control protect them from danger. To the surfer, this is the thrill of riding the waves.

Heavies, hump, takeoff and *wipeout* are all part of the language of surfing. Like all sports, surfing has its own special words.

The *hot-dogger* is a surfer who does stunts. He or she waits for the swift-moving waves. These may be only 15 feet (4.6 meters) high, but they give a short, exciting ride.

An expert hot-dogger keeps ahead of the breaking part of the wave. This is called *shooting the curl.* As the board picks up speed, the surfer moves forward. Soon the toes of one foot are hanging over the edge of the board. Surfers call this *hanging five.*

The words may be modern, but the sport itself is very old. Hawaiian kings and queens were expert surfers. They rode the waves on boards that were long and heavy. To use such boards, the surfers had to be very strong. They had to train for many years.

Things are different today. Most boards are made of plastic. Plastic is lighter than wood. This makes the boards easier to use.

People of all ages are taking up surfing today. Children learn fastest. They can't wait to ride the waves. Like the California doctor, they know they are taking part in one of the most exciting sports of all time.

Hot-Dogger

SPEAKING OF SURFING *vocabulary*

Write the numeral of each term next to the correct picture.

1. wipeout
2. heavy

3. hump
4. hanging five

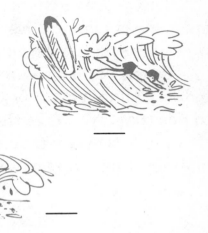

_____

_____

_____

_____

A LIVING WAVE   *author's purpose*

In each blank below, write the letter of the word the author used to make the wave seem alive.

1. A hill of water ____ after you.
   a. races   b. comes

2. A sea wave might ____ over ten stories high.
   a. stand   b. be

3. The wave ____ close to land.
   a. moves   b. is

4. The wave ____ to a peak and then breaks.
   a. gets   b. climbs

5. So it ____ the water up.
   a. raises   b. pushes

6. Hear the ____ of the water as your board slices through the wave.
   a. sound   b. hiss

☞176 • *Best Score 6* • *My Score* ____
All Best Scores 10 • *All My Scores* ____

DANGER!   *opinion*

Would you like to go surfing? Why or why not?

Key Words

junkyard
battery
radiator
engine
recycling

Old Cars Never Die

by Harland Manchester

What am I doing here in this automobile junkyard? Is this the thanks I get for having been the family car for nine years? What about all those cold mornings in the winter when I had to face snowy and icy roads? What about the hot summers when I had to stand in a parking lot for hours under a broiling sun?

I never broke down—well, almost never. I guess when one part after another wore out

and my body started to rust, my family decided it was time to junk me.

I've been sitting here for an hour. Maybe the junk people forgot me. Well, I guess they didn't. Here comes someone for me. I wonder what happens now.

Oh, I'm being driven onto a platform. Let's see how much I weigh. Thirty-two hundred pounds (1451.5 kilograms). I'm the same weight I was when my family bought me nine years ago! They will be paid by how much I weigh. Maybe being junked isn't too bad.

I spoke too soon! I don't like the looks of that lift truck with its metal arms pointing at me. What's it doing?

Hey, watch it! You're tipping me o–v–e–r! That hurt!

I think that crew of workers is heading toward me. Ouch! They took out my battery.

That's strange. They're working on me, but I'm not in any pain. It's as if I'm standing back watching them work on another junked car.

What else will they take out besides the battery? The radiator that used to keep my engine cool. The gas from my tank. The wheels and tires. If the workers keep on like this, I'll be only an engine.

I knew I shouldn't have said that. That crane standing nearby has a big magnet hanging from its arm. It's reaching for my engine. Good-bye, engine!

What will happen to my body? I'm sorry I asked. They're sliding it down that ramp into a huge oven. I guess that's the end.

Wait! No, it's not! The crane is lifting up the burned-out body and is dropping it into a long metal box. They're slamming down the lid. What's going on? The box is getting smaller. Oh, I see. The walls on each end are moving closer together. CRUNCH!

I don't believe it! I used to be a family-sized car. Now look at me. I'm a metal box about the size of a large TV set. What terrible things will they do next?

Maybe they won't do anything bad after all. Look at that. They're sending my body to a steel mill to be made into a brand-new car body. My aluminum, copper and zinc will be shipped to plants to be made into fresh metal. The rubber in my tires will go into new tires, and even the lead in my battery will be used to make a new battery.

So this is what they call *recycling*. They're saving everything they can from my old self and putting it into new cars. Who knows? Maybe the next time my family buys a new car, they may be getting me. I guess old cars never die.

WHO IS IT? *signals/antecedents*

What does each underlined word refer to?
Write the numerals in the blanks. Look back
at the story if you need to.

___ What am <u>I</u> doing here in this
automobile junkyard?

___ <u>They</u> will be paid by how much I
weigh.

___ <u>You</u>'re tipping me over.

___ <u>They</u>'re working on me, but I'm not in
any pain.

___ That crane standing nearby has a big
magnet hanging from <u>its</u> arm.

1. the family
2. the lift truck
3. the car
4. the crane
5. the junkyard
   workers

☞166 · *Best Score 5 · My Score* ___

IMPORTANT PARTS *phrase meaning*

Each sentence on the next page has one
underlined phrase. What does the phrase tell
you? Write the numerals in the blanks.

1. How?   2. Where?   3. When?
____ The car faced many cold mornings <u>in the winter.</u>
____ They sent the car's body to a <u>steel mill.</u>
____ The truck tipped the car over <u>with its metal arms.</u>

⟜54 · Best Score 3 · My Score ____

THE AUTHOR MAKES HIS POINT   *main idea*

Circle the letters of the two most important ideas in the article.

The author wanted to show . . .
- a. what happens to a car in a junkyard.
- b. what happens in a steel mill.
- c. that old things, such as cars, can be made into new things.
- d. that all cars go to the junkyard when they are nine years old.

⟜9 · Best Score 2 · My Score ____
All Best Scores 10 · All My Scores ____

WHO'S TELLING THE STORY?   *points of view*

Did you like the idea of having the car tell its own story? Why or why not? How might this story have been told by the junkyard workers? The family?

Key Words

prairie   grazing
trailer   antelope

Prairie School

"Hurry up, Eileen!" Josie said to her sister. "The other kids are in the schoolyard. Mr. Hennessey is waiting for us." Josie and Eileen ran the rest of the way to the school.

When they arrived, Mr. Hennessey walked over to the flagpole in front of the school. "Eileen, will you help me with the flag this morning?" he asked. The students watched as the flag was raised to the top of a rusty pole. Then they filed into the building to begin the school day.

18

by Andrew H. Malcolm

But this was no ordinary school. The building was a one-room schoolhouse. There were only five students in the whole school. It was a wooden shack that sat on logs. Each year, the schoolhouse was pulled by horses to a different ranch. Next to the schoolhouse was a trailer. The trailer was Mr. Hennessey's home on wheels, and it went wherever the school did.

One by one, the children settled down at their desks. They turned their faces toward Mr. Hennessey. "What story will Mr. Hennessey read us today?" wondered Josie.

Mr. Hennessey took out a book with a picture of a horse on the cover. "Oh, good," thought Josie. "It's about horses!"

The story was about a wild horse named San Domingo. The children sat with eyes fixed on Mr. Hennessey as he made the horse come to life for them. He had chosen the story for several reasons. It was an interesting tale. He knew the children liked horses. The most important thing about the story was that horses were part of the pupils' lives. They could look out the window and perhaps see wild horses grazing on the prairie. He and the children talked about the wild horses in the book and the ones they could see from the schoolhouse window quietly eating grass.

When the story was over, Mr. Hennessey said, "Now it's time for numbers." He called the class up to the blackboard. As they stood ready with sticks of chalk, he gave each of them different problems to do.

Eight-year-old Mary frowned as she tried to figure out a problem. She pressed the chalk hard against the board, as if trying to push the chalk to write the answer for her. Mr. Hennessey came over to her and guided her through the steps she needed to take to do the problem.

As he passed by Eric, Mr. Hennessey spotted a mistake in a problem. He did not tell the boy he was wrong, however. He simply said, "You'd better check that one again."

After his pupils had learned how to do the problems he had given them that day, Mr. Hennessey thought of an unusual idea for a history lesson. He told them what his school was like in the 1930s.

"Our schoolhouse had just one room, as this one does. The big difference was that it wasn't as nice. It used to be a chicken coop! I rode a horse five miles (8.05 kilometers) each day to get there. Our teacher didn't have a car, so she rode a horse to school, too."

When Mr. Hennessey finished, it was lunchtime. The class had bread and honey, grapes, cheese, soup, celery, cider and fruit. At one point, Mary and Ruth started to fight about which one of them would get an apple and which would eat an orange.

"When you get fussy," Mr. Hennessey said, "you're not hungry." He took away the fruit.

After lunch the children had recess. While they played outside, Mr. Hennessey used the free time for himself. Sometimes he wrote poems or worked on the book he was writing about wolves. Today he listened to some music tapes. He leaned back, enjoying the melodies. He thought about his job. "I'd much rather teach on the prairie than in town," he thought. "It's so quiet out here, you can hear the bubbles in a pancake break."

Suddenly Mr. Hennessey glanced
out the window and smiled. "It looks as if I
have some new students."

There in the dried grass were his new
"students"—three antelope and a rabbit.
Their heads were turned to one side as they
listened to the music.

In the afternoon the children had their English lesson. Whenever he could, Mr. Hennessey tried to show his students how the things he was teaching them made a difference in their own lives.

In the middle of the English lesson, the biggest problem for the one-room schoolhouse came up again. From under the floor came scratching and chattering. Mr. Hennessey lifted a heavy book and dropped it on the floor! The students did not blink an eye.

Mr. Hennessey had used a book in this way before.

A family of skunks had made its home under the floor. Sometimes the noise stopped the class for a moment, and Mr. Hennessey would have to quiet the skunks. Each morning the classroom had to be aired out, and for some strange reason the skunk smell always clung to the pencils.

At three o'clock Happy and Sultan came into the schoolyard. The dogs came at the same time each day. They knew it was time for the children to go home. The two animals watched as Eileen helped Mr. Hennessey take down the flag and fold it for the next morning. Then the dogs followed their masters over the hill and through the prairie grass to their homes. It was the end of another day for the one-room schoolhouse.

PRAIRIE GRASS *vocabulary*

Underline the word or phrase that will make each sentence fit the picture.

1. The picture above is of the (a. prairie, b. mountains, c. woods).
2. The animals with horns are called (a. antelope, b. buffalo, c. mustangs).
3. These horned animals are (a. listening, b. sleeping, c. grazing).
4. The children live (a. on a ranch, b. at school, c. in a trailer).

⌐→92 • *Best Score 4* • *My Score* ＿＿＿

SCHOOLTIME *signals/antecedents*

Check (✔) the correct answer to each question. Look for helpful words like *when, now* and *as.*

1. When the story was over, Mr. Hennessey said, "Now it's time for numbers."
What time was it?
＿＿＿ a. story time ＿＿＿ b. time for numbers

2. After lunch, the children had recess.
What happened first?
___ a. lunch ___ b. recess

3. The two animals watched as Eileen helped Mr. Hennessey take down the flag and fold it for the next morning.
When did the animals watch Mr. Hennessey?
___ a. the next morning when he put up the flag
___ b. while he was taking down the flag
☞42 • *Best Score 3* • *My Score* ___

MR. HENNESSEY *characterization*

Check (✔) the three sentences Mr. Hennessey might have said.

___ 1. "I tell my students if they're wrong."
___ 2. "I will move into town next year."
___ 3. "I like those silly skunks."
___ 4. "What I teach should mean something."
___ 5. "I love the prairie."
☞76 • *Best Score 3* • *My Score* ___
All Best Scores 10 • *All My Scores* ___

YOUR KIND OF SCHOOL? *evaluating*

Would you like to go to a one-room school? Why or why not?

27

Mexico's Mysterious Lost City

by David Reed

It was hard, hot work getting through the jungle. Thick vines and snakes twisted in and around the huge trees. Very little sunshine trickled down to the forest floor. Insects buzzed all around, and the sounds of wild animals filled the night.

But Alberto Ruz and his workers went on. They wanted to study how people lived long ago. Then Ruz saw what they had traveled so far to see.

"Look, there it is!"

29

THE SECRET OF THE PYRAMID

They had reached Palenque (puh-LEN-kay), the mysterious city of Mexico. More than 1500 years ago, the Maya Indians had built Palenque. But for 1000 years now, the jungle covered most of the city.

Ruz was curious about the three-sided buildings known as *pyramids*. On top of each pyramid sat a special square structure called a *temple*. Ruz and his workers made their way into one of the temples. Ruz saw a large, flat stone slab on the floor of the temple.

"That's odd. I wonder what's underneath? Let's lift that stone and see."

Ruz and his workers stared at what lay below the stone. There was a long, secret stairway going down into the base of the pyramid! The way was blocked by tons of dirt and rock heaped there by the Maya Indians.

The workers started to dig, but they realized it would take a long time. A year later, they reached the bottom of the stairway. Next they had to cut through a very thick stone wall. In the room beyond, Ruz saw something which put a chill into his heart.

"It looks like six skeletons in front of that stone door! What are they guarding?"

He cut around the stone door and stepped into a large, high room. In the center of the room lay a huge slab of rock. This, Ruz knew, was the lid of a Mayan coffin.

The workers jacked up the stone, and Ruz pushed his way under it. His flashlight knifed through the darkness. Suddenly Ruz came face to face with a human skull! It wore a mask of seashells and jade, a lovely green stone. The skeleton itself was covered with a thousand pieces of jade.

Who was this great person, so richly dressed? No one knows. But we are beginning to find out about the time in which he lived.

1300 YEARS AGO

We have learned to read some of the Maya's picture writing. From this we know that Mayan cities were used mainly by the nobles. The nobles ruled over the people.

Mayan art shows us what the nobles looked like. They wore many strings of jade beads and huge feather headdresses. Noble babies had flat boards strapped to their heads—one in front and one in back. When the boards were taken off, the babies had flat heads for the rest of their lives. The Maya thought flat heads were beautiful.

Some of the Maya spent much time learning. They wrote down what they knew. They studied the stars and the planets. From their studies, they calculated that a year was equal to a little more than 365 days.

Most Mayan people lived on farms outside the cities. But at certain times of the year, the farmers were summoned into the cities to build more temples and pyramids.

The Maya did not use the wheel, so they had no wagons to haul in the stones for the buildings. And they did not have work animals to pull the stones. People were forced to drag the huge stones from the jungle to the city.

About 1000 years ago, the busy life of Palenque came to a mysterious end. Palenque and the other Mayan cities were left empty and were almost completely hidden by the jungle.

Why did this occur? Perhaps there was no more food. Sickness may have killed many of the people. There might have been a great war. Maybe the farmers killed the nobles.

Ruz thinks we will never know the answer. Like the skeleton in the jade mask, Palenque may forever be lost in mystery.

BUILDING A GREAT CITY *summary*

What four things did the article tell you about the Maya? Write the four numerals in the pyramid below.

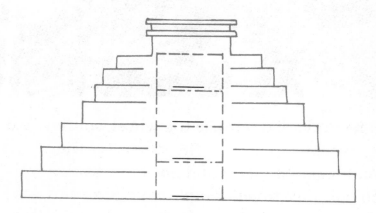

1. built cities
2. built wooden ships
3. invented the wheel
4. lived in the U.S.
5. learned there are 365 days in a year
6. studied the stars
7. had picture writing
8. had horses to pull wagons

⟜125 • *Best Score 4* • *My Score* _____

MYSTERIOUS CITY *story elements*

Check (✔) the three things that give a feeling of mystery to Palenque.

_____ a. The nobles ruled over the people.

_____ b. The city was hidden in the jungle.

_____ c. The farmers came into the city at certain times of the year.

_____ d. Alberto Ruz found a secret stairway that led to a coffin.

_____ e. No one knows why the city is empty.

⌕ 73 · *Best Score 3 · My Score* _____

MAYAN FACTS   *inferences*

For each question, write the numeral of the best answer.

What showed that . . .

_____ Palenque was empty for a long time?

_____ the Maya had wanted to keep the stairway secret?

_____ the Maya spent much of their time studying?

1. The jungle covered most of the city.
2. The Maya put a stone on the floor.
3. The Maya wrote down all they knew.

⌕ 55 · *Best Score 3 · My Score* _____

All Best Scores 10 · All My Scores _____

WHAT IS BEAUTY?   *values*

The Maya thought that people with flat heads were beautiful. What do you think are signs of beauty? What things make a person beautiful <u>inside</u>?

Key Words

patriotic
celebrating
celebration
fife, fifer
pose

The Unknown Artist

by Jo Stephens

The Spirit of '76 is
one of our most patriotic
paintings. It shows three soldiers marching for
America's freedom in 1776. Many Americans
claim the painting says more than words do
about the reasons they love their country.
Do you know the artist's name? If you don't,
you're not alone. Most people haven't
heard about Archibald M. Willard.

He was born in Bedford, Ohio, in 1836. Even as a boy, he liked to draw. He used to draw wherever and whenever he could—on walls, doors, gates and fences. This upset his parents. When he was a teenager, he got a job painting wagons, which made them happier.

When Willard was nearly 30 years old, he worked for E. S. Tripp, a famous wagon maker. Willard was supposed to paint the wagons just one color. But he did not stop there. He painted all sorts of animals and circus people on the wagons. Mr. Tripp didn't get angry, though. Thanks to the art of Archibald Willard, the "Tripp Wagon" was known all over the nation.

Because Willard had a good sense of humor, the paintings he did in those days

A.M.Willard.

were almost always funny. An art dealer (a
person who buys and sells works of art)
thought Willard's paintings were so funny
that he sold copies of them for $5 each.

A few years later, Willard drew a cartoon
called "Yankee Doodle." When the art dealer
saw it, he asked Willard to change it into a
patriotic painting. The year was 1876, and
people were celebrating the 100th birthday of
the United States.

Willard got down to work. He thought of the time he had been a soldier. He remembered how much the flag, the fife and the drum had meant to him. He decided to paint three soldiers of long ago marching to the sound of the fife and drum and the sight of the flag.

First Willard had to locate three people to pose for the painting. Willard remembered a soldier who had been his friend in the army and who had played the fife during the war. Then, at a nearby school, Willard found the person to pose as the young drummer boy. Finally Willard used the face of his own father for the tall, white-haired old soldier in the middle of the painting. The bravery and love of country in the faces of these three soldiers became *The Spirit of '76*.

People everywhere loved the painting. The city of Philadelphia asked Willard if it could borrow *The Spirit of '76*. The painting was hung in a large room so that people could look at this new work of art.

Crowds came to Philadelphia to see *The Spirit of '76*. Among them one day was the man who had been the model for the fifer. He

took out his fife and started playing it. When
the people saw who he was, they pushed so
much to get near him that they ripped a small
hole in the painting. That night the fifer

helped Willard fix the tear. Later in the year,
Willard's painting was sent from Philadelphia
to other cities to celebrate the nation's 100th
birthday.

Willard and his patriotic painting were remembered after the celebration in 1876. In 1916, when Willard was 80 years old, he rode in a car in a special parade. Three people, dressed like the patriots in his painting, marched in front of the car.

Archibald Willard died in 1918, at the age of 82. Today his name is still unknown to most Americans, but his work is not. *The Spirit of '76* lives on. What started as a cartoon by a wagon painter turned out to be America's most patriotic painting.

THESE TWO PEOPLE DID IT   *supporting details*

Underline the two facts that tell about each person listed below.

Archibald M. Willard
    a. played the fife.
    b. painted wagons.
    c. had his father pose for his painting.

The art dealer
    a. wanted to change "Yankee Doodle" into a patriotic painting.
    b. sold copies of Willard's paintings.
    c. helped Willard sell wagons to E. S. Tripp.

☞14 · *Best Score 4* · *My Score* _____

THE MAN BEHIND THE PAINTING   *fact/opinion*

Check (✔) the three words that tell you what kind of person the author thought Archibald M. Willard was.

_____ 1. greedy
_____ 2. humorous
_____ 3. mean
_____ 4. artistic
_____ 5. dumb
_____ 6. patriotic

☞83 · *Best Score 3* · *My Score* _____

WHAT DO YOU SEE? *graphics*

Look at *The Spirit of '76.* Then write the letter of the best ending for each sentence in the blank.

Sentences

1. The white-haired old man in the center has ____.
2. The artist may have used an old man, a middle-aged man and a boy to show that ____.
3. The fact that the American flag is still waving means that ____.

Endings

a. a grim, determined look on his face
b. a fife and drum
c. people of all ages were part of the fight for freedom
d. his hat raised in salute
e. the spirit of freedom is still alive

WHO DID THAT? *comparison/contrast*

Why is *The Spirit of '76* a patriotic painting? Name other things around you that could be called patriotic.

Key Words

robot
fingerprint
computer

Teacher Robot

by Andrew Radolf

Leachim is not an
ordinary robot. The day
he walked into Gail
Freeman's fourth-grade
class, the children saw he
was something special.

Leachim knows the children's names. He
tells them if their answers to his questions are
right or wrong. He can surprise them with a
trick question.

45

Leachim speaks in a tinny voice. Lights blink on top of his head. There's a window in his body. The children can see his insides— switches, buttons, tapes, wires.

But Leachim isn't a fancy toy. He's a fancy machine. Michael, Gail Freeman's husband, built the robot.

How does Leachim recognize each student? Each person's voice is like a fingerprint—there are no two alike. Leachim's computer brain has learned each student's voice. Here's how Leachim helps teach.

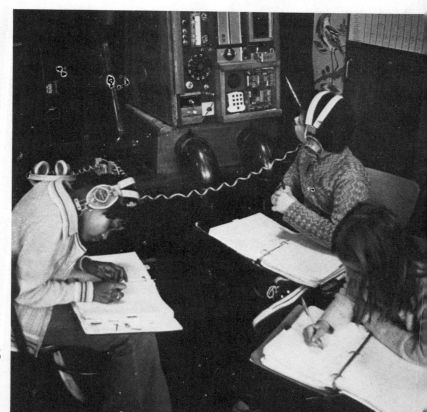

Suppose Carol needs help with social studies. Leachim asks her, "William Penn began which state—New York, Pennsylvania or Connecticut?"

Then he instructs her to press the "hold" button. That way she will have time to look up the answer in her book.

Leachim can wait forever, and he won't get angry. And there's no way you can hurt his feelings.

Carol keeps the robot waiting several minutes and then switches him on again.

"You will find the answer on page 81," he says.

Carol flips to the page and finds a map telling how each state began. Leachim repeats

the question. Carol gives him the answer—
"Pennsylvania."

"Correct, correct, you are correct,"
Leachim says.

How does the tin man know so much?
Mrs. Freeman fed lots of information into the
robot's computer. Leachim knows all the
words in the dictionary, he has seven books in
his "brain," and he even knows page numbers.

The kids in Mrs. Freeman's class want to
learn from Leachim. It is more interesting to
look up a word when you can press buttons.
So the children learn two things—the word
and how to operate a machine.

A robot can never replace a person. A
robot can't give you a hug, for example. But a
robot is good for a
boring or dangerous
job. Like waiting for
you to make up your
mind. Or screwing 100
screws into a car. Or
working with red-hot
steel. Leachim even
makes children laugh.

SWITCH ON THE ANSWER *generalizations*

Check (✔) three things that are true of most robots, not just Leachim.

Robots . . .

___ 1. can't walk.
___ 2. are machines.
___ 3. get tired.
___ 4. have computer "brains."
___ 5. can do different kinds of jobs.

☜77 • *Best Score 3* • *My Score* ___

INFORMATION ON LEACHIM *cause/effect*

Each sentence below is missing an ending that explains how Leachim works. Circle the letter of the correct ending.

Leachim knows the names of the students because

a. the children tell him their names.
b. he knows their voices.
c. he knows what the children look like.

Leachim knows lots of things because he

a. makes tapes of what he sees on TV.
b. reads books that he thinks are interesting.
c. has a computer for a brain.

Leachim won't get angry because

    a. machines don't have feelings.
    b. he is very nice.
    c. his students usually know the right answers.

☞52 • Best Score 3 • My Score ____

OUR NEW TEACHER   *fact/opinion*

Two sentences below are facts. The others are opinions. Mark A for each fact. Mark B for each opinion.

___ 1. The children could see Leachim's insides.
___ 2. Leachim knew the students by their voices.
___ 3. Everyone liked Leachim.
___ 4. Leachim was special.

☞86 • Best Score 4 • My Score ____
All Best Scores 10 • All My Scores ____

ROBOTS—HELPFUL OR HARMFUL?   *evaluating*

What can a robot teacher do that a human teacher can't? What can a human teacher do that a robot teacher can't?

Key Words

metal
thermometer
mercury
furnace
system

A House That Runs on the Sun

by Blake Clark

B A N G! Mr. Thomason looked up at the sky. "I hope it rains. Maybe a storm will cool things off."

Just then thunder boomed again, and rain spilled from the sky. Mr. Thomason dashed to the barn. As he ran through the doorway, drops of water from the roof fell on his head.

"The water from the roof is warm!" Mr. Thomason said. "I wonder why. The roof is dark in color. I know that dark things soak up light and heat very well. The roof is made of metal. I know that things made of metal like heat. The dark metal roof must have soaked up the heat from the sun!"

Mr. Thomason waited in the barn until the storm was over. After the sun had been shining for a while, Mr. Thomason got a thermometer. He wanted to see how hot the sun had made the air under the roof.

The air was so hot that it made the silver in the thermometer push past 140° F (60° C). Ping! The heated mercury broke the thermometer!

Mr. Thomason thought about what had just happened. "Maybe there is a way to catch and hold the sun's heat. The heat from the sun could heat a whole house."

That is just what Mr. Thomason did. He and his family built a house that runs on the sun.

First they made the metal roof. They painted it black and covered it with glass. Then they put a big tank of water in the

basement. They ran a pipe from the tank, up the side of the house and onto the roof. They put in a small pump to send the water through this pipe and then ran the pipe along the top of the roof. They made small holes in that part of the pipe so that its cool water could flow down the roof and become hot from the sun's rays.

Next the Thomasons stretched a gutter along the bottom of the roof to catch the sun-warmed water. The water would go from the gutter into another pipe. This pipe led back to the tank in the basement.

How did the Thomasons get this hot water to heat their house? They put rocks all around the outside of the tank. The rocks would soak up the heat from the hot water in the tank. Now the heated rocks would warm the air around them. The Thomasons set up a small blower to force the heated air out into each of the rooms.

At last the Thomason home was completed! The family moved in on a sunny day in October. The next two months were

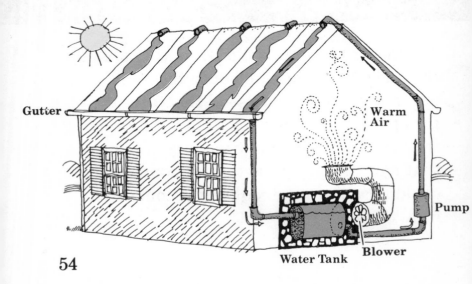

Gutter

Warm Air

Pump

Water Tank

Blower

cloudy and chilly, but the house was heated by the sun. It was not until December 21 that it was cold enough for the oil furnace to go on. It stayed on for just 15 minutes. Then the Thomason's sun-powered system took over again. It did most of the heating for the rest of the winter.

The Thomasons did more than heat their home. They heated their indoor swimming pool for six months. They turned their sun-powered heating system into a cooling system during the summer.

Can your home be made to run on the sun? Probably not. It would cost too much to rip out the old roof and put in one made of metal and glass. However, it does not cost a lot to add such a system to a house you are building.

The Thomasons were not the only people to build a sun house. Other people feel that using the sun can help solve problems. It can heat buildings without making the air dirty, and it can also save oil and gas. So by helping with these problems, sun houses like the one the Thomasons built may be like a bright light at the end of a long, dark tunnel.

HOW DOES THE SUN HOUSE RUN? *cause/effect*

Put the sentences below into the order in which they happened.

_____ The rocks are warmed by hot water in the tank.

_____ The hot water is piped from the gutter back to the water tank.

_____ Cold water is pumped from the tank, up the side of the house and onto the roof.

_____ The sun's rays heat the water on the metal-and-glass roof.

_____ The blower sends the warm air through the house.

SUNNY FACTS *supporting details*

Draw a sun (☀) next to the fact in each pair that helped Mr. Thomason come up with the idea of building a sun house.

_____ a. Fire needs air in order to burn.
_____ b. The sun has great heat.

_____ a. Dark things soak up heat.
_____ b. Light things reflect heat.

_____ a. Metals come from rock.
_____ b. Metals like heat.

_____ a. Rocks soak up heat and warm the air around them.
_____ b. Hot air rises.

_____ a. Mercury spreads out when heated.
_____ b. Mercury is silver in color.

☞130 · *Best Score 5 · My Score* _____
All Best Scores 10 · All My Scores _____

A BRIGHT IDEA *sentence meaning*

What do you think the author meant when he said that sun houses may be like "a bright light at the end of a long, dark tunnel"?

The Remarkable Desert Zoo

by Jean George

Key Words

desert
lizard
museum
chuckwalla
cactus

U.S.A.

Arizona

New Mexico

Desert Museum ★

MEXICO

I watched the funny little lizard scurry across the sand. Sand is a problem for you and me. But not for this lizard.

A very thin skin dropped over her left eye. It tossed out a grain of sand. Her upper jaw came down over the lower one to keep sand out of her mouth. Her fringed toes were like snowshoes because they let the lizard walk on the soft sand without sinking.

A SPECIAL ZOO

I was watching a fringe-toed lizard in the Arizona-Sonora Desert Museum. All the animals and plants there can be found in that part of the country.

These animals have had to make themselves fit in with the hard life of the desert. The pretty kangaroo rat never drinks water. Its body gets enough water from the seeds that it eats.

When I visited the desert museum, the first thing I saw was a huge "bowl" filled with lizards. One of the lizards was a chuckwalla. Something scared him, and he darted into a crack in the rock. He filled his body with air until he was too fat for anyone to get him out. If he were in the desert, this would help keep him from becoming another animal's dinner.

As I looked around, I saw that the zoo was really a very small desert made by human beings. The animals play, sleep and eat in homes just like their natural ones. They live in buildings and out in the open.

THE "TUNNEL"

Where do the animals go when it gets too hot in the sun? The zoo has a "tunnel" to answer this question. Here, below the ground, are dens for desert animals.

Many desert animals stay in their dens during the daytime. When I pressed a button outside each den, a light went on inside, and I could peer into the animal home. I saw bats sleeping upside down. Foxes rested and

groomed their fur. Snakes stretched out in the cool air. I pushed another button to view cactus roots.

MR. MOUNTAIN LION

There have been many animals in the zoo since it opened in 1952. But the best loved was a creature named George L. Mountainlion. He liked to show off for the people who came to the zoo.

William Carr started the zoo. He was also a writer for a newspaper. His stories were written as if George, the mountain lion, were writing them. These stories brought hundreds of people each day to the zoo to see George.

One day George died. That night Mr. Carr wrote George's last words. They can be found on a stone at the side of a trail at the zoo.

The stone tells how George felt about his human friends. It says that he left them all the sights and sounds of nature. To humans who were tired or sad, he gave the quiet and peace of the desert. To the children who heard him purr and watched him play, he gave laughter and joy. And last, he gave his own happy spirit and love for others to those who remembered him and his museum. It was there that he did his best to show people that he really did like them.

Every day the desert zoo helps people to enjoy the gifts George left them.

WHO'S THERE? *supporting details*

Circle the names of four animals and plants you would find in the Arizona-Sonora Desert Museum.

1. foxes   4. bats

2. snakes   5. seals

3. polar bears   6. cactus

☞123 • *Best Score 4* • *My Score* _____

STAYING ALIVE *classification/outline*

Match each animal with the way in which it has learned to live in the desert. Write the letters in the blanks.

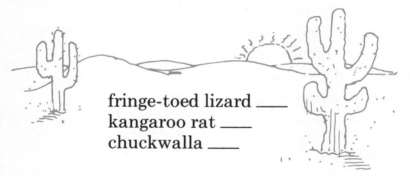

fringe-toed lizard _____
kangaroo rat _____
chuckwalla _____

a. hides in a crack in a rock and fills its body with air
b. has no problems with sand
c. gets all the water it needs from seeds

☞52 • *Best Score 3* • *My Score* _____

DESERT LIFE *main idea*

Check (✔) the three most important ideas in the article.

____ 1. Animals have to make themselves fit in with the kind of land in which they live.

____ 2. Plants don't belong in a desert museum.

____ 3. All desert zoo exhibits should be from nature, not made by human beings.

____ 4. The desert is a hard, dry land with no beauty at all.

____ 5. Animals like George L. Mountainlion show people that the desert museum is more than just a zoo.

____ 6. The desert museum brings people and nature together.

☜82 • *Best Score 3 • My Score* ____
All Best Scores 10 • All My Scores ____

A MUSEUM OF YOUR OWN *observation*

Pretend someone asked you to start a nature museum filled with things around you. What plants and animals would you choose? Give reasons for your answer.

64

Key Words

disk
plastic
flying saucer
wrist
champion

Monika Lou,

Magician of
the Flipped Disk

by Wallace Wood

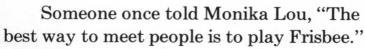

Someone once told Monika Lou, "The best way to meet people is to play Frisbee."

"Play <u>what</u>?" Monika asked.

"Frisbee. You know. It looks like a plastic plate. You zip it into the air, and it spins along like a flying saucer."

The basic
Frisbee backhand

The overhand
wrist flip ▶

So Monika bought a Frisbee and walked to the park to try out her own "flying saucer." She turned the plastic plate upside down and held it out just in front of her. Then she gripped the bottom of the disk with four fingers and placed her thumb on top.

Monika tried to toss the Frisbee into the air. But the plastic disk headed straight for the ground. She picked it up and tried again. Sometimes the wind swept it to earth, but Monika kept trying.

A young friend came over and said, "You've got a pretty good arm with that Frisbee. But you're not snapping your wrist when you make a throw. Here, watch how I do it."

The boy tossed the Frisbee with a flick of his wrist. The Frisbee spun and skipped over the air. "Now you try it," he said.

Monika tried to copy his throw. The Frisbee twirled out for a long distance and

gently landed on the grass. "It's <u>beautiful,</u>" she gasped.

This was the beginning of Monika's love of Frisbee. She went to the park every day to practice. People would stop and watch her or speak to her. Some wanted to play Frisbee games with her. She learned many different ways to throw and catch the dancing disk.

Today Monika Lou has made lots of friends. And she has done something else. She won the title of women's long-distance Frisbee champion of the world. Her winning throw with the 4.203-ounce (119-gram) disk was an astounding 83 yards (75.90 meters).

To keep in training for her sport, Monika practices three to five hours every day. She does the backhand, two-finger shot and overhand wrist flip with ease.

Monika says, "You don't use just your wrist or your arms, but your whole body. The way you move affects the way you throw."

67

The thumb throw

Distance throwing isn't the only kind of Frisbee sports event. There are contests for the best aim, the longest time the Frisbee stays in the air and freestyle. In freestyle Frisbee, the disk is thrown back and forth between two people. The throwers are judged as much on their graceful style as they are on the kinds of throws they use.

There are even different kinds of Frisbee games people play. One type is called Ultimate Frisbee. The Frisbee is passed from player to player, and a winning toss is finally sent across the goal line.

Another kind of game is known as Frisbee golf. A player tries to use as few throws as possible to get the Frisbee to land in a basket that is set up far away.

If <u>you'd</u> like to start tossing a Frisbee around, begin with the basic backhand. Then you can learn the other throws. Maybe you won't become a world champion like Monika. But you just might make some new friends.

REMEMBER HOW? *graphics*

In the blank under each picture, write the numeral of the name of that Frisbee throw.

1. two-finger shot
2. overhand wrist flip
3. thumb throw
4. basic backhand

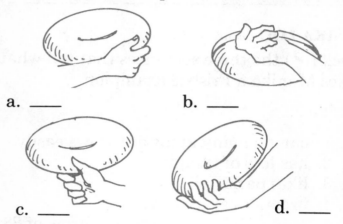

a. ___

b. ___

c. ___

d. ___

🔑105 • *Best Score 4 • My Score* ___

THE NAME OF THE GAME *classification/outline*

Draw a Frisbee (⟷) around the name of the event each player is describing.

"My Frisbee stayed up for over 16 seconds!"
    a. longest time in air   b. most throws
    c. highest throw

"Our team won the game with a great throw over the goal line."
    a. Frisbee tag   b. Ultimate Frisbee
    c. best aim

"My Frisbee landed under the trees on my first throw. But my next toss sailed right into the basket."

a. freestyle   b. distance   c. Frisbee golf

☞49 • *Best Score 3* • *My Score* ____

MONIKA LOU   *characterization*

Check (✔) the three sentences that tell what makes Monika a Frisbee champion.

Monika . . .

____ 1. can do many kinds of throws easily.
____ 2. has lots of friends.
____ 3. likes parks.
____ 4. practices every day.
____ 5. made a winning distance throw of 83 yards.

☞76 • *Best Score 3* • *My Score* ____
All Best Scores 10 • *All My Scores* ____

MAKING FRIENDS   *opinion*

Why do you think Monika Lou made friends by playing Frisbee? Can you think of other good ways to meet people and make friends? Give examples.

Key Words

bubble
plaster
revolving door

Bubbles Are Beautiful— And More

by Wolfgang Langewiesche

Is this horse going into a garage? No, not at all. Look at the next page, and you will see that it is walking into a very different kind of building.

71

The horses are part of a school—a school to teach people how to ride. Today class is being held indoors in a building known as "The Bubble."

Bubble? The building is in the shape of a bubble. If you look at its "walls," you will see that they are made of cloth, not wood or metal or plaster. So what holds up the building? Air!

How can air hold up a building? Think
about what happens when you blow up a
balloon. You force air into the balloon, and
the air presses against the sides until the
balloon is blown up.

The same thing happens in a bubble
building. Blowers fill it with air, and the air
holds up the walls.

The horses had to enter "The Bubble"
through a double garage door. People enter a

bubble building through a revolving door. A regular door would let air escape, and the building would slowly go flat.

Why might you want to build a bubble?

One reason is that a bubble is much cheaper to build than a regular building.

Also, its fabric is tough enough to walk on or to withstand strong winds.

If you want to move, just let the air out. Then fold up your building and take it to a new place.

A bubble can be just about anything you want it to be. It can be a tennis court, a bowling alley, a greenhouse, a storage shed, a grocery store, a football field or even a house.

If you stand inside a bubble, you will see that the light shining from outside makes the smooth, curved walls glow softly, like a lamp. You can order bubbles in different colors or with stripes. You can even have a window (one that doesn't open, of course). Yes, bubbles are beautiful!

FILL THE BUBBLE *supporting details*

Only five descriptions listed inside the bubble support the main idea written on the outside of the bubble. Circle those five descriptions.

Bubbles are both useful and beautiful.

1. cheap
2. many rooms
3. tough
4. colorful
5. easy to move
6. many uses

☞168 • *Best Score 5* • *My Score* _____

DIFFERENT OR ALIKE? *comparison/contrast*

Check (✔) the two items that are true <u>only</u> of bubble buildings, not regular buildings.

_____ 1. air holds them up
_____ 2. windows
_____ 3. useful
_____ 4. withstand strong winds
_____ 5. easy to move

☞ 32 • *Best Score 2* • *My Score* _____

AIR POWER *generalizations*

Circle the letters of the three things below
that need air inside them to make them work.

a.   b.

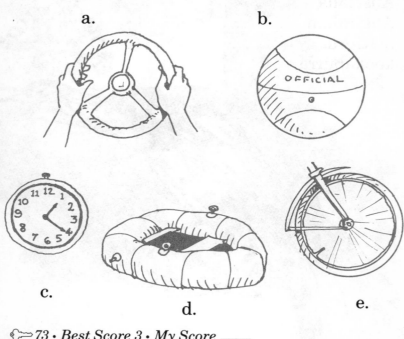

c.

d.

e.

73 • Best Score 3 • My Score ____
All Best Scores 10 • All My Scores ____

BUBBLES, BUBBLES, BUBBLES   *awareness*

What kinds of buildings does your town or
city need? Could bubbles do the job? Why or
why not?

Key Words

marvelous
lyrebird
Australia
Australian
platform
kookaburra

James, the Marvelous Musician

by Ambrose Pratt

Mrs. Wilkinson stared out her window. In her garden stood the most unusual bird she had ever seen. He was small and brown. He was about the size of a chicken, but he had a very long neck. His black eyes shone.

The bird's tail stood high in the air. In fact, it was taller than the bird himself. Its feathers spread out in the shape of a harp.

It was then that Mrs. Wilkinson knew what sort of bird had come into her garden. It was a lyrebird. The lyrebird gets its name from the shape of its tail, which looks like a lyre, or harp. The lyrebird lives only in Australia, where Mrs. Wilkinson lived.

Mrs. Wilkinson went to the door and spoke softly to her visitor. "Hello, boy, hello."

The bird seemed ready to run away from her. Mrs. Wilkinson did not want to scare him, so she did not go too close to him.

When the bird saw that Mrs. Wilkinson was not going to harm him, he started to look for breakfast. He scratched with his feet through the leaves that lay in the garden. After an hour, he had eaten enough bugs and worms. He glanced at Mrs. Wilkinson, and then he spread his wings and glided off into the jungle.

Mrs. Wilkinson called, "Good-bye, James. I hope you come back and visit me."

James did. That same day, at sundown, he flew in. Mrs. Wilkinson stepped into her garden. "Hello, James. So you like my garden, do you?"

James peered at her with his black eyes.

"Go on. Have some dinner. I won't hurt you."

The sound of her voice calmed James. He carefully overturned a few leaves with his feet and dug for worms. When he had his fill, he flew off.

And so it went. Twice each day, James came at the same time into Mrs. Wilkinson's garden. In the beginning, he was ready to fly away at the least hint of danger.

As time went by, however, James got to feel so safe with Mrs. Wilkinson that he would tap on the living room window each morning to let her know he was there. She built a small platform for him to perch on just outside the window.

Mrs. Wilkinson found that there was something more unusual about James than the shape of his tail. It was his voice. One morning when Mrs. Wilkinson was in the garden, she heard his calls as he flew in from the jungle. He landed on his platform.

She said, "Hello, boy."

"Hello, boy," answered James.

He could talk!

Next he opened his beak and let out a low laugh. The laugh got louder and louder until it sounded like the call of the Australian kookaburra (kook-uh-BUR-uh) bird.

As the last note faded, he began a new song filled with the calls of more than 20 birds. There were other kinds of sounds in his song, like the tooting of car horns, the rat-a-tat-tat of a jackhammer and the bark of a dog.

After a while, James got tired of making sounds from the world around him. He started dancing to a song of his own. Forward and backward he went. He crossed his feet just as if he were a person. His dance ended with three quick steps, and he folded his tail like a fan.

James became more of a friend than a pet to Mrs. Wilkinson. One morning she slept late. James came to her garden at his usual time. He tapped on the living room window as he had always done. But Mrs. Wilkinson was still in a deep sleep.

A few hours later, Mrs. Wilkinson woke up and wondered, "What is that scratching noise?"

A small head popped up at her bedroom window. It was James! When he saw her, he broke into the most beautiful song Mrs. Wilkinson had ever heard. She got out of bed and looked outside the window. Then she understood what had caused the scratching noises. James was not tall enough to peer through the window. So he had scratched together a mound of dirt on which to stand.

Later that year, Mrs. Wilkinson learned something even more wonderful about her lyrebird. James was a teacher of music.

One day he arrived with his mate and their babies. James gave one of the young lyrebirds a voice lesson. He began with the call of the kookaburra. Over and over, he gave the sound. Over and over, the young lyrebird practiced the sound till he could do the complete song.

When scientists heard about Mrs. Wilkinson's friendship with James, a group of them came to visit Mrs. Wilkinson. They wanted to study her lyrebird. James came soaring in from the valley. He landed on his platform.

As the scientists watched, James fanned out his tail. The feathers flashed with black, brown and purple. And as James began his song, he cast a spell on the scientists who listened to him.

And so it is with the lyrebird. Its sounds are filled with joy, and its magic touches the hearts of all who listen.

NAME THAT BIRD *supporting details*

Pretend you have just seen a strange-looking bird. Put a line through two details below that would tell you the bird you have just spotted is <u>not</u> a lyrebird.

1. It is about the size of a chicken, but it has a very long neck.
2. Its tail looks like a harp.
3. It cannot fly.
4. It eats fish.
5. It can sound like other birds.

☞*24 • Best Score 2 • My Score* _____

HIGH-FLYING WORDS *figurative language*

The author made you see, feel and hear many things about the beauty of the lyrebird.

Circle one of the sentences in each pair below and on the next page that the author used to tell you about James.

How his eyes looked:
    a. His black eyes shone.
    b. He had black eyes.

How he left:
    a. Then he spread his wings and glided off into the jungle.
    b. Then he flew away into the jungle.

How his tail looked:
   a. He had a lot of pretty colors in his tail.
   b. The feathers flashed with black, brown and purple.

☞47 · Best Score 3 · My Score _____

MR. JAMES LYREBIRD   *characterization*

Check (✓) the five words or phrases that would describe James if he were a human being.

____ 1. trusts strangers
____ 2. takes time getting to know someone
____ 3. is a good friend
____ 4. hard-working
____ 5. mean
____ 6. music-loving
____ 7. not interested in music
____ 8. sad
____ 9. spends time with his children
____10. lazy

☞172 · Best Score 5 · My Score _____
All Best Scores 10 · All My Scores _____

JAMES AND MRS. WILKINSON   *inferences*

What did Mrs. Wilkinson do to win James' friendship and trust? How did James show his friendship for her?

86

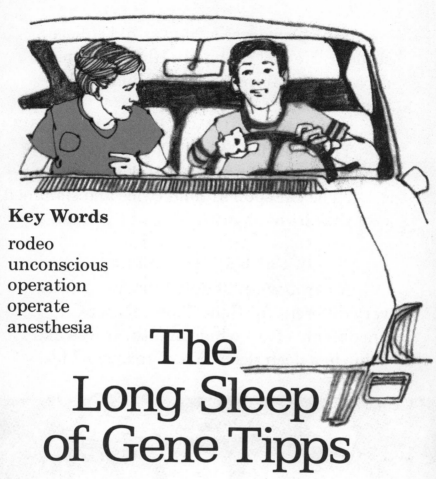

Key Words

rodeo
unconscious
operation
operate
anesthesia

The Long Sleep of Gene Tipps

by Joseph P. Blank

"I think the calf roping was the best event in that rodeo, Gene," said Ricardo.

"I know. I didn't think that cowhand was ever going to get near enough to rope that calf."

Gene Tipps was a 20-year-old college student. He and his buddy Ricardo were driving home from a rodeo—and then it happened.

"Gene, hold on! We're going into a skid!"

Their car had hit a slick place on the road. Ricardo turned the wheel, but it did no good. The car spun around twice and slammed into the dirt bank at the side of the road.

GENE'S LONG SLEEP

Ricardo wasn't badly hurt, but it was very different for Gene Tipps. He was unconscious for a whole month. It was like being in a deep sleep. When he opened his

eyes at last, he didn't know his parents or his friends. He didn't seem to know or care about anything. After three more weeks, the doctor said to Mr. and Mrs. Tipps, "We can't do anything more for your son. You'll have to take him home and care for him there."

Six months went by. Gene was still only half conscious. If he was left alone, he would sleep 20 hours a day. He would not speak, except to answer yes or no. His parents had to talk him into doing almost everything.

Mr. Tipps would say, "Gene, it's time to get up."

Gene just lay in bed.

Mrs. Tipps asked, "Gene, did you hear what your father said?"

After about five seconds, their son slowly formed the answer, "Yes."

"Don't you want to get up, Gene?"

"No."

His father wrapped his arms around Gene's shoulders and propped him up in bed. "Come on, Gene. Make an attempt."

Gene simply stared ahead. His mother came to the side of the bed with a walker. A walker is a metal frame that is similar to a table with no top, and people who have trouble walking use it to lean on.

Gene's parents helped him stand. He leaned heavily on the walker.

"Gene, please try," Mr. Tipps begged. Slowly Gene dragged his right foot a couple of inches forward and put his weight on it. "Now, the other one. That's it."

Soon Gene could move with the help of the walker. The same slow steps had to be

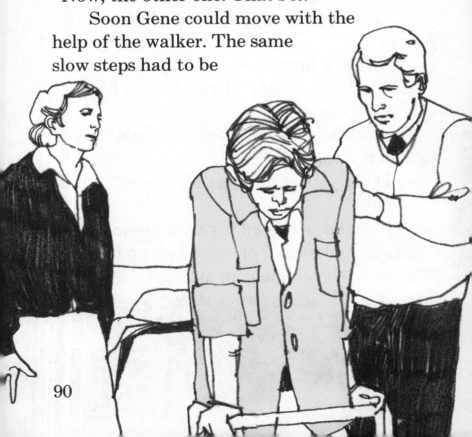

taken with other things. His parents had to teach him how to shave, comb his hair and brush his teeth.

Mr. and Mrs. Tipps would not give up hope. They made Gene learn to walk on his own. They took him for walks and drives. They made him use his body, even though he hated to.

Mrs. Tipps left the TV on all the time. Something there might catch Gene's interest, she thought. Gene stared at the TV set for hours. But his long "sleep" went on.

LIFE OR DEATH?

Then Mr. and Mrs. Tipps found out that Gene had to have another operation. The doctor warned Gene's parents, "I will have to give Gene anesthesia. The anesthesia will put him into a deep sleep so that he won't feel pain when I operate. I don't know what effect anesthesia will have on Gene. He may not come out of that deep sleep, and he might even die."

The operation couldn't be delayed. Mrs. Tipps remained at the hospital with Gene. He slept for a long time after the operation.

LIFE!

When he awakened, it happened.
Somehow, in an instant, Gene became once
more the person he had been. He stared at his
mother. Why did she look so much older? He
did not understand that it had been eight
years since the car accident.

"How long have I been in the hospital?"

It was the first question he had asked in
all that time. Now his mother stared. She
answered carefully, "Three days."

"Three days? I'd better get back to
college. How long have I been out of school?"

Mrs. Tipps had waited for this for so
many years. "Is the change real? Will it last?"
she asked herself. She tried to be calm as she
answered him. "Well, son, you've been out of
school for quite a while." She put her hand on
his arm. "Gene, are you awake?"

He sat up. "Why, sure, Mother."

Mrs. Tipps spoke slowly. "Gene, the last
time you were really awake was eight years
ago. You were in a car accident."

The words didn't make sense to him. "I
can't believe it!" Gene tried to think back. "It
seems that I was very sleepy for a week or

two. It seemed that you and Dad were always trying to wake me up."

He had so many questions. How were his friends? Who was head of the country now? Then he asked, "How's that piece of land Dad bought?"

"We had to sell it to pay the hospital bills."

Gene's face grew sad. He realized the grim truth of the last eight years.

The doctor came in. Gene smiled and asked, "What did you do to my head?"

The doctor was too astonished to joke. She had never seen anything like this before. It was like the difference between night and day.

THE NEW GENE TIPPS

Soon Gene was able to go home. He couldn't see as well as before the accident, but he was excellent at learning and at solving problems. He was ready to go back to college. He could use recorded books till his eyes improved.

Why did Gene go into his long sleep? Why did he come back from it? Doctors don't know for sure. Some say he was helped by the anesthesia used during the operation.

Gene is thankful for the love and help he got from his mother and father. But Mrs. Tipps has her own way of looking at it. "It's we who give thanks. Gene has come back to us. That will always fill us with wonder and excitement."

REPORT ON GENE TIPPS *summary*

In each blank, write the numeral of the missing word or words.

1. rodeo	5. conscious
2. glad	6. operate
3. fight	7. anesthesia
4. brain	8. a blood test

Gene and Ricardo were driving home from a ____. After their car crashed, Gene was half ____ for eight years. Then the doctor had to ____. The doctor gave Gene ____ so he wouldn't feel pain. Afterwards Gene got well and was ready to go back to college.

125 • Best Score 4 • My Score ____

WHICH ONE IS GENE? *comparison/contrast*

The difference between the Gene Tipps who was half asleep for eight years and the normal Gene was like night and day. Put 1 before each sentence on the next page that describes Gene when he was sick. Put 2 before each sentence that describes him when he got well.

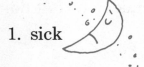   1. sick      2. well

_____ He wanted to go back to college.
_____ He needed a walker to get around.
_____ He sat in front of the TV for hours.
_____ He made jokes.

🔑88 · *Best Score 4* · *My Score* _____

WAKE UP TO THE IDEAS   *main idea*

Check (✔) the two most important ideas in the article.

_____ a. TV can help people get well.
_____ b. If you go somewhere, always take a friend along.
_____ c. It's a good idea to own a piece of land, because you can sell it if you need money.
_____ d. Don't give up hope.
_____ e. We aren't thankful for the simple things in life until we lose them.

🔑31 · *Best Score 2* · *My Score* _____

All Best Scores 10 · *All My Scores* _____

SIMPLE THINGS   *empathy*

Do simple things like walking, writing or tying your shoes. Do them as s-l-o-w-l-y as you can. How do you think Gene felt doing such things so slowly?